Lights On The Way Out

poems by

Diana S. Adams

Finishing Line Press
Georgetown, Kentucky

Lights On The Way Out

ACKNOWLEDGMENTS

Corrupt Press published a chapbook titled '*Catch*' containing seventeen of these
poems in 2013.

Green Zone, ed. Larry Fagin created 300 copy edition pamphlet
containing 12 poems from this manuscript

'Confession', 'Surfacing', and 'The Empress'—*Wave Composition*

'Continuum'—finalist *Fish Poetry Prize,* anthologized in *Fish Anthology*

'Opening', 'A Pack'—*Mipoesias*

'Composer', 'Bat', 'Lights On The Way Out'—*Pataphysics, Five New Things*

'Horizon', 'Blanketed'—*iArtistas*
'Corpse Flower', 'Winter Interior'—*40 Below, Edmonton's Winter Anthology*

Publisher: Leah Maines

Editor: Christen Kincaid

Cover Art: Dylan Harris

Author Photo: Amy Adams

Cover Design: Elizabeth Maines McCleavy

Printed in the USA on acid-free paper.
Order online: www.finishinglinepress.com
        also available on amazon.com

Author inquiries and mail orders:
Finishing Line Press
P. O. Box 1626
Georgetown, Kentucky 40324
U. S. A.

Table of Contents

IV.

I

Inventory of Effort

I find a book in the grass
The Book of the Self As an Ox

I dream a stone boat
two people paddling

I smell the accident
before it occurs

blood & flowers
my house is a mess

mirrors function
as interruptions

How long must I plow?

Horizon

Your sweater is browner
than sparrows
you wear it to go unnoticed
   & lie in the grass
hidden as a cellar
to do your math
sure, the future is coming
but upside down
& outside in
 I become a nun
earth is half burnt
the sun is asleep
& you layers array
what the new colors are

Monody

I hear the bird's three notes
         a little set of steps
to a place at the back of my atlas
where autumn is shaking
& radiant with no vertigo
I try to stay itinerant
to feel lighter than paper
but I make the mistake
of rearranging the notes
to come descending
into the burn
of an empty field

With Airglow

there's always a bit of light in the sky
after sundown & before stars
a perfect self would notice it
sit on the steps & jot out notes
then create it in a laboratory
a blue luminescence
arcing over a Victorian street scene
where ladies of the evening
assume their corners
I'm so busy with business
I get lost
lined up at the lunch truck
& when I'm alone at night
eating my macaroni
I see all the spaces
where I'm supposed to be

Pickings

An arm appears
in the radish patch
broken mannequin
& a grey dog
pretending to be lost
a dead lady drinks beer
staring in wonderment
they have all fallen
through a partially open door
the novelists forgot to lock
they're always dropping things
I pick them up & wash them off
the arm at least offered
to lend a hand
yet those obnoxious novelists
keep changing my name

Continuum

At the border I forget who I am
so they turn me back
I move to a new state
& attend lectures on cosmology
I get a job at a market
piling up produce, gutting fish
but I watch the clock
thinking about time travel
& being a tourist of the future
where I could eat tortellini
& teach myself to repeat
in a world without hinges

Indeterminate

An undersized steak on an oversized plate
edged with ivy

My daughters think up names
for the receding light
Brian? No, Amy says, it's Fleecy

Above everything
are a few true things

The bears in the bear department
pause to sniff the same light

Each scene moves with its questions
not eager for answers

Red Fences

The fences never existed
but I was prompted to blurt out
the first thing on my mind
& now that they're here
I feel better about myself.
The color is potent—dare I say
Newmanesque Vir Heroicus Sublimis?
Why not? Let's go with that
& in this demented afternoon light
I can serve my guests appetizers
with aplomb & a sense of primary
importance. Forget what you learned
in school. Take your shoes off.
Make the whole thing up.

Surfacing

The sun arrows the road
that I am building for you
curved like an arm
with transparent surface.
You were elusive in love
women with black horsehair
raided the rooms
drinking Riesling, eating nuts
smoking, expecting sex.
Please release them
down another road
At night I drive alone
sucking on cloves.

Half Full

Today ends, colour
without design

no walking no coffee
no bacon no piano

dear tongue, you might
find a star in the pantry

pigeons do their night
commute, their one concept

rests between
boredom and skill

I profit from impeccable
dress, memory

and a mirror. The phone rings
I pretend I'm in the right place.

Kind & Strange

A hand came out
of the book she was reading
fingers pale and wrinkled
pointed at her
then at the door
don't question it
she thought & went out
with the book closed
the hand was a bookmark
she bought food and cigarettes
& ate a ham sandwich
they stayed out in the spring sun
patted a dog nearby
& the dog licked the hand
the hand said *I've been lost*
it poured her a glass of wine
& stroked her hair
that hand was a good man

The Empress

The fortune cookie said yes
you are an empress
but I hate ceremony
I'm better suited
to other forms
a flake of snow, for example
a candy dish
or a mango, & yes
you are a penis
dragging in the dust
but who is that bright light
crashing on the window?

II

The New Agenda

I had the theater people over
to paint our house
blue chartreuse maroon
the walls have nothing to do
with us, what a relief
& through the many purple doors
they've added anterooms
to invite people we don't know in
so we can have a few moments
previously impossible

    *

Just so you know
in this particular house
you must wear a hat
so we can spot you
when you enter into conversations
I've put out some leaves
in the garden
& inked in
lawn chairs and trees
the woman in the corner
has been installed to laugh politely
keeping us positive
life itself has a way
of clogging progress
remember your violin?
it kept moving forward
following the logic of music

    *

I've arranged for a moment
out of *Mansfield Park* candles at the pianoforte
Fanny looks dumbly at the woods
& her heart shakes with rapture

this happens in the green room
people are carpooling over
a car will damage a tree
that's okay, how it is supposed to be
everyone gets a chance
to be in on it
before removing to the smorgasborg

Scheduling Disasters

We planned to go for a walk
but we are here at the burnished doors
of Masterpiece Theatre with an audience
of butlers & chambermaids
hoping to be called up
to be part of a murder.
Today's special is duress
so we won't feel bad
about killing each other after coffee. I'm
cautiously optimistic
there will be blood
& semen on my red dress,
is this 1895? What a relief
we're not here anymore.

Nose to the Mirror

What you are not going to see:
young woman
   green violets
    disfigured birds
so help yourself to a peach
watch yourself eating in the woods
rotate each breast
spin them as you please
some guy's going to come climbing
the vines, polite as a butler
I'll be out on the couch
with a new wig & an hourglass
preparing myself
for better mirrors

Autobiography

Later I find the spot
where I was dropped as a baby
& hence became a mutterer
I could only do figure sevens
on my hypothetical bike
& I argued with supermarket fruit
disappointing my tapeworm
my father was a butcher not by choice
I am the master of my house
but that is all
when I hear the pipes
of long ago clanking I cry
the shadow of my hand on the wall
in the shape of a pork chop

My Mud

There's mud on my lens
mud on the scenes to come

when I get stuck I unmake it
disassemble a table, for instance

things have a way of re-arranging
other things except us we are a mess

when the mud takes over, I'll travel
back to where we first met

Lights on the Way Out

This galaxy makes me thirsty
I was hoping for a darker ride
with a few turrets
these cities could have been ordered online
all heads huddled over the same book
for me it's different
I like my light grainy (ecru)
with fighting in the refectory
& powerful storms
that shake the bricks
& freeze the candles
cities in black
thinking is technology

Blanketed

Throw out all your sweaters
time is talking
as the smell of Galliano
drifts out of the cemetery
listen to the historic ticking
telling you to take in guests
so you won't be alone
with the pack of cards
Aunt Dick gave you
decorated with wolves
collaborating over a rabbit
what does that mean
I don't know but I know
there's potato chips in that scene
& you will feel blanketed
by the dog's nails
clicking on hardwood

Corpse Flower

People admire our Virginia creeper

asleep at extreme degrees below

& crowds line up to see the Corpse flower

putrid at best, it's diapers & death

at the indoor botanical garden

also known as the misshapen phallus

it has a purple rod three meters high--

let not bother with eerie flowers

my mother owned a funeral home

& father became head embalmer

to impress her, to get her

by tapping fluids, painting faces

stuffing dead limbs into new clothes

once he put red hair on the wrong person

another time a body groaned

as the casket went into the ground

it popped the lid & sat up in the January drizzle

they said it was gas

no wonder he became a geographer

Off Topic

I like orange, you answer
when asked how it's going
that's a superb answer
from an otherwise
conversation vacation
close your eyes, depose the pain
here's a month
with oysters, an extended moment
including a long drive
through delirious fields
we lay out our blankets
where waxwings drunk
on mountain ash
whip up the air
an unseasoned place
without neighbors or acquaintances
so your wired mind can reach the
rest of you

Shaping

Lost in the topiary
of a perfect world

I fake it at work
& weep on weekends

Fish glitter in the tank
their eyes are wild balloons

Something nuzzles me inside
everything is a thing

Hook

Between a hook
& ladder

there's air, the go-between
element, the space

where your opponent
runs in black

& loses. All malediction
is useless

Perfect Spot

There are herons here

& later there will be more

I will add spiders

dog about to bark

I will not allow any voices

there are too many already

the lake is composed of difficult curves

it would have been simpler

to begin with a small pond

the dogs and a few flies

I call it Mylandia

& no one does anything here

it's better that way

III

Who Does She Talk To?

The man outside is asleep
under a tree
a crack in the window pane
upsets her, she is economical
even her name is plain, Ann
His name is Itsuki
ocean in Japanese
when will he wake up?
she almost drowned him
in the backyard pond
she talked to herself
turning it another way
to become another day
without a pond
rock at the window

Water's Edge

I love the view
but the fish move too slow

take a look
this is you, for now
bobbling along

with me you're convincing
by yourself you are a fool
this will pass

when four bearded men
carry you out
for a spell

you will emerge large
no, not grotesque
leonine comes to mind

Hardheaded

How many swords will it take
how many onions
to get your head out of that trap
you locked yourself in
if there's a road in there
continue on it
but you won't see
the apples in stalls
the winter daisies
that are almost invisible
& smoke off the lake
in the shape of a hand
you need a window now
or a skeleton key

Asea

On deck you can see

all around yourself

& still be in character

the sun cuts through

& beats the rugs of your head

you get delirious

watching whales

expecting sex

where there's only water

Jumble

We picked at a salad
I was looking for something
trapped in your interlocking sentences
of course it wasn't there
I don't even know what I want
we had camaraderie
shuffling into the evening
over what you call Arroz con Pollo
which is bits of chicken mixed in rice
big deal, I'd prefer a large Dagwood
and a liter of lager, two for you
to be honest the truth never helps
buy hopefully it will be there
when we finally grow up

Variety Pak

A debut fruit appears
at Tha Kha floating market
I follow its idea
out of a rain barrel
for once I'm not bored
I divide my time
with machetes
seeking the egg-shaped bulb
with spiny eyes

                *

The metal rooster
spins counterclockwise
I mistake the snow
for an argument
it's dry snow
so there's hope
for carte blanche
I eat without thinking
or accounting for
who will be right
in the next life

                *

When I wore my bells to bed
I conjured a menace
all black keys depressed
these exaggerations are pleasant
to think without words
once a bear came
to a seance
looking for garbage

*

That pirate ship is
either under repair or
up for sale "as is"
The pirate must be a thinker
I follow his gaze
out to sea, trying not
to make too much
of bobbing corpses

Bear Headquarters

I gave it a try, it was worth it

as a bear I was baronial

I plashed in the water

Mrs Owen, my piano teacher

didn't bother me anymore

I saw greens no human has seen before

I will have to pay for this

it is being added on as we sit here

not speaking

you on the sofa, numbed

with a glass of something

listening to the city

the good thing is

I don't care

brown is in

Not Much

Deep inside the pressure
to do better
you have a way
of sitting at an angle
& licking your lips
another olive disappears
the joy of paradox
trapped between cat & bird
it doesn't take much
to get out a little more
but your head was made soft
by bricks that fell
every other day

Confession

I love basements

plastic fruit too

there's no sense of here or now

I was a prisoner

at my mother's parties

peddling liqueurs

mopping up spills

I moved to my aunt's

she lived in fear

of god & fat

& was hurt in church

kneeling on a nail

after an affair with the priest

my own affair is my affair

it is as old as our daughter

Begotten

How did your mind
become another mind?
maybe you should tell them
just a paragraph
even the dirt is eager for it
the ropy legs of relatives cross
& uncross at Christmas
the stuffing is lethal
tell them about the light in the barn
& the bees' metallic racket

Episode

A truck drove into her mind
black and sleek
why are you here?
go to the edge of town, it said
there are flowers in the snow
she picked the flowers
ate cheese, drank scotch
but it was parked between her eyes
please leave!
after a few minutes
she stopped asking & rested
her dead boyfriend
overcome with reverence
made space
they both fell asleep
so peaceful

The New Life

She revised the view from the train window
to get somewhere else
arriving at a park
with all the problems of moderation
it was the color of her eyes
the light narrowed
the air was hot

He would disappear and reappear
they will find the hotel
& lie nicely
when the bed evaporates
they will sit in the cut grass
& he'll say *you're the color*
you're the color

Vacation Place

Feeling my elements
I think up a lake
blue is good for me
but not ducks
ripping up the parchment
with cranky honks
you love ducks
& could be one too
or more
where's my calculator?
all your sides
interrupt mine
I'm so glad I packed
my fragile knives

                    *

You missed the boat
& got caught
sucking on a life jacket
please read the rules
no rowing
no sucking
the blizzard is here for a reason
beware of the squirrels
they're not organic
& programmed to attack
when faced with smiles

*

A mosquito tries
to land on my head

& keeps me near sleep
hope-like & blank

its buzz is a piece
of the continuous present

& reminds me
 I'm a murderer

Catch

The experimental self-portrait
is a disaster

spindle hair & man hands
back flab

I root out something interior
by blowing up the mouth

my eyes remain uncarbonated
bringing off the unthinkable.

Bat

little umbrella
with a hell fetish
dried-up
on the shower floor
the dog ate you
like a potato chip
you could have been
my kid brother

IV

Curiosities

1.

People say I'm strange
OK! I say
it's all I've got going for me
pull up a chair, take a look
this pen is from the moon
that umbrella came from
who knows where
interstellar space
I stand behind my rubbish
If you have any questions
I'll be out in the solarium
enough is not enough

2.

The emperor wears calico pants
in the All-Happy Garden near Peking
he orders steamed turtle
I sit at his black lacquer table
I'll take a steak thanks
my apologies to the cook
who reminds me of my mother
I long for a nap
in the grass near the river
he insists I try the white cherries
covered in snow
to help me forget
how I came here
in silk boots and a fur collar
like a baboon

3.

He sleeps with his mouth open
welcoming mosquitos
another attempt to revolt me
it's so dark I can't see my arms
so I go out dancing
my partners' eyes are taken
straight from the painting
in the anteroom
blue saucers
they stay with me all the next day
while the emperor sleeps

The Composer

The man in my dream
hands me a hammer

it reminds me
of coconuts

too bad he's based
on a photograph

in the police museum
a young man

murdered with a meat cleaver
& stuffed in a freezer

part of his brain
under a simal-focal microscope

revealing his musicality
his notes on copulation

his fear of disappearing
before singing something

Winter Interior

Invent a lake if you must

but it'll be gone by tomorrow

you have to shake hands with the ice

before it crawls into your head

there used to be a another door here

a juggler walked through it

never left, he can't juggle

now there's heaviness between us

in what's left of the house

it's so cold we threw out

what we thought we wanted

Biography

Every cloud is a continent
　　　　you know this is not true

it's just a product
of the vertiginous forward thrust
of thought

Thought is a clock
many things are clocks

one has a bit of you inside

your face, all egg-like
behind the moving arms

tentacles hiding your inner anger
hunger & doubt

Sightseeing

I don't want to hear about it
colon cleansing
names of ships
lost in the Bermuda Triangle
your hatred of the color red

It's my turn to complain
I've been everywhere
& gotten nowhere
falling into canals
between hotels
unreflected in every window
even in Vienna
walking around without a name

Your blood must be black
or worse *fulvous*
I sit in this chair
all night eyes open

The Invisible Man

I saw the invisible man
in the drugstore
counting out pills
hey, man
I heard you last night
moving around in my room
our arrangement was for *me*
to touch *you*, to see
if you were coming or going
or just playing hard to get

Nevermind

I asked what he was doing
then realized he wasn't here yet
that's okay there's time
he's still out walking
on some planet
looking for jokes
I'll wait in the garden
& complain for awhile
get it all out
otherwise I'll wind up
doing nothing again
I found a few jokes myself
in that book he wrote about grackles
he knows his birds
he acts like one too
foraging in garbage

Planet No. 9

It's a real planet
they have invented
I go there once in a while
to sit on the stone steps
they pay me
with another currency
for a more secure future
it's cold and blurred
no one seems to know where
they're going
all roads lead to weeds
one woman spits sunflower seeds
at me & asks rhetorical questions
she leaves me alone only
when I pretend to be dead

North

It takes a movie to remind you
where you're supposed to be

bare shouldered at a gas station
on your way out west

something in your watery-brown tea
allows for a moment in the middle of now

between here and there, a flicker
here being a supermarket café, in a toque

maybe if you changed direction
when you were ten

& followed the glinted hints by the road
instead of taking the shortcut home

Driving without a Car

I did it with my eyes
took in the road
let it out again
there were a surprising number of dogs
waiting to be walked
a woman sang as she walked through the trees
houses were chalky or luminous
I tried to thank someone for everything
the odor of milk & dust
on the cuffs of my new suit
I liked looking at my hands
gripping the wheel
which was my forehead

Predella

In one panel
I'm chopping wood

in another I'm asleep
on a pile of garbage

wearing an earthly crown
made of cabbage

ever the louche, leering
over a platter of pickled herring

or pulling faces
on our country's coins

my ears are detached
inattention is my regimen

Attend

I take your temperature
with my fingers

a ghost clinic opened
hoping to be known

fever is a skillful drifter
its edges & unused music

move the air above
but you won't get far

Diana **Adams** is an Edmonton, Alberta based writer with work published in a variety of journals including *Boston Review, Drunken Boat, Fogged Clarity, Oranges & Sardines, The Laurel Review, Ekleksogaphia.* Her work has been included in several anthologies including the *2009 Rhysling Anthology.* Her third book of poetry *Hello Ice* was published by BlazeVOX Books. Corrupt Press published her chapbook *Catch.* Larry Fagin published a chapbook under the same title with some of these poems. Diana has three poems in *Best American Experimental Writing 2016.*

www.ingramcontent.com/pod-product-compliance
Lightning Source LLC
Chambersburg PA
CBHW021200090426
42740CB00008B/1174